SOME MURMUR

SOME MURMUR

LYDIA UNSWORTH

for F

Text copyright © 2021, 2024 Lydia Unsworth.Typesetting and book design
copyright © 2024 Downingfield Press Proprietary Limited.
All rights reserved.

Without limiting the rights under copyright reserved above, in accordance with the Copyright Act 1968 (Commonwealth of Australia) no part of this publication may be reproduced, stored in or introduced into a retrieval system, or transmitted, in any form or by any means (electronic, mechanical, xerographic, recording, or otherwise), without the prior written permission of the copyright owner and the publisher of this book, except for brief passages quoted for the purpose of criticism or review.

Lydia Unsworth asserts their right to be
known as the author of this work.

Cover and book design by M. G. Mader.

ISBN 978-1-7635569-0-4 (paperback)
ISBN 978-1-7635569-1-1 (e-book)

First published 2021;
Acquired and published July 2024 by

Downingfield Press Proprietary Limited
Suite 346 / 585 Little Collins Street
Melbourne Victoria 3000
Australia

For a full list of addresses and contact information, visit
global.downingfield.com

Downingfield Press undertakes its work on the unceded lands of the Wurundjeri people of the Kulin Nation and pays respect to Elders past, present, and emerging.

 A catalogue record for this work is available from the National Library of Australia

PROLOGUE

I moved to Amsterdam five-and-a-half years ago, ten days before the Brexit referendum, an act of relocation that felt like running along a path in a computer game and having the tiles fall away, burn up, or turn to dust behind me. I remember seeing one of those spoof newspaper articles at the time that said: *SHOCK NEWS: THOUSANDS OF BRITONS REALISE THEY ACTUALLY LOVE THEIR COUNTRY*. And that felt very true; I was in love and there were things I had taken for granted. For example, an ease of being in a space; a way of inhaling the fresh, damp air after the rain; feeling connected to the history of a savoury pie eaten out of a plain paper bag on a northern-bound train. It was the physicality of the landscape I was after, the self of the groundstuff, the traces of ancient hardships that lay low in the architecture—the context by which I had been shielded and into which I had grown. Waking up to the result of that referendum felt like something had abandoned me, or me it. The details were uncertain. The evaporation of a parent. Like looking away for a moment and then looking back to find out that everyone is gone. Like the landscape wasn't mine anymore. It never had been. Something had been there all along murmuring under the surface. Something that I thought I understood but that had in hindsight never been a part of me.

When I found out I was pregnant, not long after the Brexit referendum, it felt like a part of me had died and like a second part of me was steadily dying. I don't want to sound ungrateful, because a lot of people feel a lot of things about procreation—about wanting babies, not wanting babies, really wanting babies, having babies, not having babies, really not having babies, how you should have babies, how you should not have babies—but the way I saw it, from that side of the expansion, was that some unknown and unknowable event was lurching towards me, and its manifestations were showing up all over my body; rising out, bearing down.

And this unknowable event, irreversible and now unstoppable, was a passing through. A ritual test of endurance. The black hole that was forming inside was gathering matter, gaining momentum, and I was being sucked in and shrunken and replaced. Matter begets matter. I was physical, becoming more so. Various parts of my body on various days were taking on the properties of stone or lead. The internal world rather than the external was where things were taking place, was where the news was, the threat.

As when approaching a black hole, time stretched out in the countdown to the birth, and nothing that I was able to directly comprehend or observe lay over the border. Months and then weeks and then days consumed the whole of the future. Despite the crowds of people likely to be enduring childbirth at the exact same moment I was, I was alone and inadequately prepared. There was, perhaps, a future—others had survived the fall, many had passed on their stories—but I wasn't able to believe in it.

As when approaching a black hole, a part of me went through unscathed, floating for what seemed like lifetimes in the anonymous nothingness beyond. Until we were officially a mother and a daughter: two sacks of lack and muscle: a call and a response. As when approaching a black hole, a part of me remained scattered, motionless: stretched across the surface of the event horizon as a growing heat began to engulf me in flames.

Given enough time, the black hole will radiate away its mass, and vanish (the child will grow, the host will deflate). No energy is ever lost, and so all exertions eventually tend toward something other. Toward something or other.

You are still who you were before, you are exactly who you were. But you are also something else entirely. You have been sawn in half and paraded across a stage in two wooden boxes, choreographically twirled around, and set in motion. Your two dancing halves have been clicked back together and the saw has been removed (*ta-dah!*); the lights flick on and you stand up and there is no real proof that any of this ever happened. The baby slides to the ground like an animal, grows from the ground like a plant, iridesces like some rare mineral.

Like a Mother Writes

In fragments of one-handed time we survey the day's
impressions. They put the injection in the left arm, always
taking blood from the left arm. 'Which arm
do you write with?' Like a mother writes.

I lift heavy with my left side. Baby-monster on left hip.
A ledge. It grows with him. My model slant,
my catalogue twist.

I write with whichever side I am not feeding with. Left-
handed phone type. Phone held in air above baby's head.
Phone swiped behind back as baby's eyes move over to that
other life.

Which is your dominant side?

Stay put, baby. Comply.

Stoop

The body bends towards you like a plant. You are
my sunshine, my ray of sunshine. What do you call
a plant warped by circumstance? I hold you up to the light.
Ten lifts then ten to the side. Environmental stress weakens
the plant. You are heavy fruit. My stem turns to you,
hulking sunflower head bows down, seeds fall from my
eyes. Wind-blown tree – frozen in flight. Umbrella inside-
out, novelty tie coat-hangered into a U-turn, leg kicked out
high. Flamboyant ice. Waiting for a coin in a hat to say
it's time.

Kyphosis

postural
　kyphosis
　　is
　　　rather
　　　easily
　　　corrected
　　　with
　　　education
　　...
　slouching
poor

posture

leaning
　back in
　　chairs

　　children

　　carrying

　　　feeding
　　　　children

Shut Up and Drive

I shut myself up
like a sea anemone
when the world poked me
    said no thanks
and allowed a small fissure
to enter my body
    we don't decide
so much as we let our guard down
and lax
slack
all merry from the giving up of it
we root for the flood
    and the flood wins

good on him I said
  someone said it was meant to be
and I grew like a cubed watermelon
or a cat-in-a-jar meme
and my head filled itself
with thoughts of me
 when shit hits the fan
inside your own body
the rest of the world
  dims

I walked in ever-decreasing circles
until the circumference of the known world
was equal to that of my own
    the calendar made no sense to me
all this supposed future
all this physical autonomy
 I shut myself up like a sea anemone
    steepled my hands above my head
and contracted my body column
    ducked inside
    I bowed to my successor
extracted from the tight throat
of falter at the junction
    so far so successful
    in his drive to be

The First

squeals in like a toboggan
hot dart of love
manipulation
to secure her place
at the public premiere
of this helpless
threatening sequel
my deer on the late-night through road
lost and blinking at the approach
of this new planet we are all trying to land on
  stubborn comet eyes
floody with revelation in the veering headlights
tight knot of will you love me
  so hands in the sun
  so neck-deep in ocean
  so furious hailpour
  so avalanche of huff
like the baby orangutan holds
the mother orangutan holds
the branchless tree
in her bulldozed forest

Babymoon

we are going to space
we are strapped in though she has fought against it
first she tried to take the ride untied
but the experts they were for once united

there are so many checks and procedures

they say you can only love
a thing when you have broken
through the pain barrier

I said send me send me don't mess around
send me I want to have this baby

so we all shot off on the date imposed
closed our eyes and fists and put our heads
between our knees and held our noses and said
that we were going to like it

there is no air up there the food is dry and unfamiliar

you come out of your room at night you orbit
me whenever I am holding it

I bat you off like I would tiny flies heading for the
only source of water

and the spider she is tidying up that's right

and the fox who steals the chicken
she is only prepping what she needs for dinner

and the girl who goes to space
says if I don't make it display me in this open coffin
all right we say and sign
and we think nothing further of it

but all the little buttons had more colours
than we had names
and all her little fingers were out there
slamming on the quartz

and we saw the planets how they all tried to resize
and the sharp red moon that yawned and sighed
and our hands were tired, tied
from having set the thing in motion

the gates to the park were open

I had carried home so much baby
and sought to make it mine
that the swarm of flies that was my child
slipped from out my sight and out the sight of
all these whirring satellites

when I looked to the sky I could have sworn
I saw you making a harp out of bones

Attachment

It's a telephone,
my child says, *so, no,*
you cannot share my biscuit.
Nana's game is abruptly ended.
The child, though against pretence
in certain role-play, proceeds to kiss
the screen and in so doing obscures her face
from the province of the in-built camera.
These telephone kisses are not returned
due to the vast cultures of bacteria
commonly known to be breeding
on the surface of such apparatus.

INDUCTION

the procedure in itself is not painful, though some may experience it as pain

On the first evening we took the three bags and the car seat and left the flat. Descended the communal staircase. I wanted to walk so the transition from here to there felt appropriate for the scale of the event. We walked three bus stops then waited and went by public transport which eventually took longer than the walk would have. This way it wasn't our fault.

On the first night we took the three bags and the car seat and returned home the way we came. The journey felt quick, the transport connections were all in our favour.

On the first morning in the thin air we took the three bags and the car seat, despite not fully believing in the baby yet, that it would breathe, curl, dream its way back to the flat through this taxi-jam world. And we walked. A walk that took place behind the scenes where the angled sticks supporting the buildings' facades catch on the wheels of the suitcase you're pulling along. You remember travel. You remember previous selves you've since diverged from.

On the first morning in the waiting room we took the three bags and the car seat and looked like we owned the place. Dropping things down wherever we liked, loitering by the water dispenser, swirling paper cups.

At the end of the first morning we took the three bags and the car seat and made our way to the room named Belize. We were shown around. Told not to go out. We found convenient places to drop the things we were carrying.

On the second evening we took the three bags and the car seat and shoved them in a corner. We were brought coffee, a menu of six meals to choose from, we pulled the chair-bed out. Every movement of a table or a trolley or a cushion revitalised us. We could be at home here.

On the second morning we didn't take the three bags or the car seat anywhere and this pleased us. We experienced relief. I rummaged in my personal bag for far too long and inefficiently; I hadn't unpacked, didn't, knew I wouldn't, and this frustrated me. I am very good at not quite committing to a space.

On the third evening we didn't look at the three bags or the car seat. I stuck my hand deep into the main pocket without much consideration of the gesture, pulled out the items I thought I would need over the next few hours. I sweated through the blinking night in the clothes I had arrived in. There was little point.

On the fourth morning the three bags and the car seat made me feel sad and tired. We needed to act. I consented my body to the women in blue uniforms and face shields. It was the logical next step. But it was also an interruption; a part of us had already chosen our meals from the menu for that evening.

On the fourth evening we took the three bags and the car seat and were told to go home again: freed, if temporarily. Convalescing. We ordered a curry, watched a comedy, no thoughts beyond these minor impulses.

On the fifth morning we took the three bags and the car seat and booked a taxi to the hospital. There was no more space to construct this narrative. Journey was delay. Pilgrimage without purpose. I wanted quick fixes, transportation, painted backdrops unravelling when I flicked the lights.

On the fifth morning we took the three bags and the car seat and returned to the hall with the named rooms, to embark on the first morning once again, this time in California. We put the three bags and the car seat in the corner of the room and reminisced about our previous visit. It amused us how this room was an almost mirror-image of the room we'd had before. Like going to a neighbour's house and sensing how things might have been. We pointed at disposal units, incubators, toilet brushes and laughed, expected the staff to laugh with us. We commented on the colour scheme, stated a preference.

On the fifth evening we looked at the three bags and the car seat and didn't notice the slowness of our movements.

On the sixth morning I cried and I cried until they made it begin.

On the sixth evening, after so much swimming, the other side was reached.

On the seventh morning we took the three bags and the car seat and put the baby in.

Transformation Anthem

I map my own body in the shower:
desert, quarry, earthquake.

I form swift new waterways, geysers of you,
sporadic yet spectacular, in every room.

I am frozen into news item – an exclusive scoop.

The limb is amputated, grows itself a whole
new body.

I walk as if I still have meaning, as if I still own
the right to all this space.

I am a hot-air balloon landed, felled on its side:
that state of billowy mid-deflation.

I am a slim tarpaulin in a heavy gale.

I leave the house, enter a topography of chance: eyeing the
backstreets for some morphology to call my own.

I try to run but all the little children on scooters
are scooting so quickly away.

The Pulling

I'm still a child, I tell my child. A girl, she says, like me. We are two girls, she says dancing. The other, with his merfish tail, raises a slow tortoise neck at the sister pinball. We are two hundred thousand girls, I say, more, and here in this country in Europe we are entitled to twelve weeks leave of absence with our remora-fish babies. Twelve weeks to unhibernate, to learn to love eternal demand.

Frantic tadpole legs kick me awake as the night-mauve sky stagnates. My eyes, omnipotent pools of misheard order. Thoughts on the verge of lost jump into my water-throat as I dream of free-standing kitchen islands, running around and around past closed cupboard doors, chasing the fuse-burn untied balloon that is my let-go-of daughter.

Our running slows. We rest our remora heads on the tiled floor between grasshopper flecks of past-onion and post-garlic. A sound leaks from my working organs: Tell me you'll tend to me as I tend to zero.

You are not my best friend, she says.

Zeppelin

obsolete, in the middle of a field
selling vintage portraits of myself
saying please remember me

Attempts to Recover My Previous Form

Pilates /
I raise one arm up and over the head. Accept the hip. Curl. Tell me I'll change. That my body is a cavern. Rolling, sweeping hills. A wind sock in a long, deep wind. Every crack, every click. Completion.

Zumba /
The one man was there again. The back of his vest dark with sweat from a previous body-pump class. The hall is well-lit with padding along the wall where I drop my bag. I stand at the back, and noticing it is a substitute teacher for the third time, wonder how many classes I will need to attend before I know what to expect here. This week we don't do any thrusts, instead this teacher's choreography is heavily focused on shaking the tit line. I look at the one man in the class every time we do this. He is absorbed.

Pole /
Bruises on arms. Body heavy on the floor. Vertical attempts to get over, to be impossible. Body introvert in floating. Never touching, never going up or in or down. Body spins like a recently shelled electron, out on the nth, alone with the pole, nobody knows you are here.

Flex /
The mats are laid in a circle. Knotted hammocks hang from the ceiling and there are glasses filled with candles on the floor. This makes it easier, the droops of fabric, the low light. After a while I begin to look at the faces rather than the leggings of the other people in the room. We stretch one leg in front and one behind us, the latter bent and pointing up as far as we are able to persuade it, aided by a belt looped around the ball of the foot and pulled, loosened, pulled over our corresponding shoulder. We have to create more room. We repeat the exercise hanging in the looped hammocks, bringing the rear leg off the floor, top half of my body slopped across my bagged leg like a corpse.

Zumba /
Feet are the laughing stock of body. Jumble of misstep fluke and turn and don't ever find yourself at the front with your butt half-twerk and round and round and round with the hips. And there, between wall-size window and mirror-size wall I am learning how not to see my surface. Pounding legs into floor and fist and elbow back and pumping water action and something about this is so sincere. I can't even crawl. Thirty-something in a church basement and being told how to crawl.

Zumba /
The lights are low and I have opened my legs far and wide for the substitute teacher. Some of us might not be able to make this movement – that's okay. Keep your head up high. I notice the texture of my hair as I curl my hand around the uppermost arc of me. Five, six, to the beat now. These are the times. Send a shock through your legs from the centre. Convulsion. Turn like a sensual stroke of yourself. Be panther.

Box /
The reason isn't important, triggers are often small. The triggers are small but often. I punched the bag.

Pilates /
Thought it was wise to stand before the mirror crack, wide like bags of old receipts in supermarket bins. I didn't compare myself to anyone but how can you not look at all those upended trunks trying to hold their bad weather in?

Pocket of Love

Sitting quietly in the undergrowth waiting to be seen. Small bubble of no twigs, no leaves and a pop when you unfold in. Comfortable circumference. Pocket of love. But no hands. No ant colonies, tubes of commuters, railway of words in unstoppable protrusion over stand-at-the-back, body-punch body-punch. Aerosol cans are bad for the mood, a vicious spray, hard against skin. Is it still a chance you had if you couldn't rein it in? Keep your head down, silverfin, under you go, no support in the wild group water. Potentials hydrating immaterial soundscape. The illustrated tower, the fox, long fingers of a pianist. Hard to believe *are you a dancer?* is a question once asked of me. Back when I could get a stick around my body like no one else could tame the thing.

We Demand Floating Structures

I have appeared on the paving without geometry, equator.
They say the rain brought me out. They say my house is
flooded, the carpets thick with recent history, solemnly
documented. They tell me my walls are leaking: wall-front
dripping over wall-surface until occasional pyramid, and
me spilling out of it like escape from a funnel.

The paving slab is grey and wet and I am pink and soaking
also. Too meandering for disguise, too sluggish to place a
bet on my own survival.

The land around me is not anyone's, hardly land,
dull reflection, creeping tide, stone thrown into lake and
wobbling murmur. I belong underground, with the others
who belong underground by my side.

I came here for celebration, for a widening of mind. Instead
this melting. Plastic bowl in ball of heat, flattening and
losing reticence. I sliver to a halt and search for a crack in
the belly-up of my own demise.

Individual Lots

Every day we harvest whatever
has poked its head above ground. We eat.
Shave it all back to zero. For many months
this system of replenishment has been enough.

Every morning I find the ground risen,
I put on my shoes and stamp the trail back down.
Rats are undermining the furniture,
the building blocks of life.
My heavy tread doesn't solve the problem,
but I can make it look as if it didn't happen.

Objects keep arriving as we try to empty
the rooms. We are finding objects
on the street, winning objects in local lotteries;
it is hard enough to stop buying.

When I see a space, I lie down. An empty car park
exfoliates this body I have been prescribed.
The uniformity of the individual lots
as simple as breathing out and in. The noise
of windswept foliage attempts to drown me.

Escape

was the place we were after – cool flint against close to the bone. The hole to the cave led through to the most open section of quarry, wide earth contained and held. Too tight to chance it, I lingered around the opening, hoping. Watching the other bodies, unflinching, while I, with all my future children, left hanging around until the world felt known. Hunger like an animal. Hunger like one piece of criticism and ten years later and then dead. Cranes tug at the stitches of cities. We sink into spark notes of selves unled. I remember the sun at close quarters, all over us, and we thought this was the place to spread our deck chairs and our lilos and everything we'd ever thought of – legwarmers, visors, all reasons to adore us.

In The Corn Field
(2011)

It happens that there is a child running through a heaving swaying mass of corn. The corn stands higher than the child itself, is more complete and more richly developed. The child's face is pink against yellow, beige against green. The midday sun makes everything incriminatingly visible.

A giant voice is behind the child. Child is skipping away from our conceived gaze. Voice is behind us, behind our disembodied 2-D character. Voice is loud, booming.

Voice, although deep, is muffled and slow. It is decreasing in tempo with each syllable, dragging. Voice warns child not to enter the competition. The child will obey.

Child is running and skipping, is in a different world to voice. Corn protects child with its warming enormity and child goes on, ripping off an ear, twirling it in hands or before face, discarding it, claiming another. Voice is slow and loud and threatening; the child will not betray it. Voice envelops child in its frequency, slowing until it resonates, until bones of child are shaking with deep, low sound-waves. Child fears and is lifted out of playful wonder. Child is halted and knows the fear of the world.

Child is snatched out of time's continuum for one brief and everlasting moment. The frequency is more than words, the slowing. There is meaning in the deceleration, awful truths the child cannot yet comprehend.

Child knows fear and child knows rebellion. Child buys a ticket because this is the only way to be strong. Child knows the chances of winning are minimal, has basic concepts of probability. In buying a ticket the child learns risk, danger, protest.

Booming voice is still beckoning in background. With ticket in hand, child runs, flees. Corn field could not be emptier, less useless, or more fragile. Child flees. But there is no chance that child will win. Child would not be singled out among many, because child is nothing, no one. Voice and ticket and irreversible actions haunt the child. It considers consequence and shivers in the steady one-way traffic of time.

The thing is done. Child learns worry. Irrational worry in the face of statistics. And the child learns guilt, is paralysed by fear. Voice repeats, is looping round and round in mind of child, until new sound forms and expands out of the distance.

New sound is melodic, uplifting and final, lifting cheer straight out of the fat brown earth. New voice is death's own messenger, oblivious. Child cannot share in the joys of the world. Child looks down at number on ticket. New sound is reading out its improbable digits, destroying the world.

Child has put an end to everything with one rash gesture. It cannot be taken back. Voice will be listening. Voice is unseen yet always within earshot. Child cannot hide. When it does not stand tall and go to collect prize, new sound reads out child's full name. Ears of corn and ears of father are one and the same.

Child runs as voice beckons to it, a deafening wail which deepens and spreads to infinity.

Specific Ways I Will Apologise to My Children

For example, I'll leave a note on the stairs outside their wobbling apartment next to a small piece of dropped plastic where they're bound to notice as they bound away. Huge arrow pointing to the end of the world. Or I'll write it in fridge poetry using only the leftover and available words: Honestly Nothing Memories Love Saw What Honestly Nothing Flood I Okay Talk Drinks Tremble. Or I'll send them an office email. Thanks for reaching out, but I don't have the capacity to raise you today. You pose some great questions, and I'll follow this up as soon as my workload abates. Or I'll run a marathon in their name. Or I'll clip a lock around a bridge rail and toss the key into the river into the sea onto the seabed because what difference does it make? Or I'll fly to them wherever they are and say it to their face before I take a slapdash tour through their new world and fly straight back again. Or I'll bake them a cake, homemade, throwing all the harmless packaging away. Or I'll buy them high-street clothes they can call their own, for all their generic bodyshapes. Or I'll tell them a story, as long as I am old, of everything I was ever told or have thought and not known how to say, and I'll hope they'll listen to some of the tones, hope the sonar won't drown me out, hope that the songs of lives cut into and hung above our own can still drip a little onto such full plates.

MOTHER

The mother slips away. She is seen leaving the room, sliding her arm out from the pool of sweat at the nape of a neck time and again. She is a GIF of leaving. CCTV footage of the precise moment of abandon.

The mother falls inside herself because it is all she knows. She remembers wide days of context, complex arguments (though there are still complex arguments, rigorous lines of questioning, word sharks, pivotal statements on which hang entire futures). She writes this on the toilet, knowing her eldest has learned to unlock the door.

The mother spends all day wanting to write. She wakes up eager for the day's end. Those hours of reading and writing that must come, that will surely come. Her child is talking to her and she is only half listening. The other half of her attention is projected forward, toward that hubbub of evening logistics: the food, the clothing changes, the washing, the hoarding into bed. She is moving pieces of the puzzle around trying to find the quickest route out of the maze.

She is on the phone writing poetry. On the phone again. She has RSI for poetry. Insomnia for poetry. She needs WiFi for poetry. Disrupts her melatonin for poetry.

The mother wants to sleep, but here she sits scrolling. Uninterrupted, pretending this inertia is *me-time*. She has grown so used to demand that without it she is stagnant water, potpourri.

She is sleeping. Trying to. She has moved the children and the computer and is repose on her own mother's bed. Sirens blare, a narrowboat displaces water, territorial bird call, distant traffic, a honk, a far-off cry, a HGV reversing. She has left the window open, for the air, for the union! Her eyes are pinballs, skittish visualisers. She gets up to lock the door. She lies down. She returns to her computer.

The mother is woken at hourly intervals throughout the night. She is kicked and beaten. Small purple bruises rainstorm her chest and arms. Indigo pebbledash of dug-in nails, of *come to my aid*.

She fears interruption, balloons popping, doors opening, loud strangers, centre tables, live music, hands clapping, goals being scored, people to one side trying to get the attention of people to the other, alarm clocks, the volume of mid-programme advertisements, a draft touching skin, lights-out, lights on, low batteries, erratic machinery, her phone ringing, even a text.

Just one hour alone and she is awake. A dream between two sprints.

She would like her actions to be without meaning or consequence. A series of vignettes. Only colour, noise and a soft fabric flapping past her open face.

The mother wants water, water. A woman in the soft play offers her water. *Wait, you are feeding, aren't you?*

The woman in labour reverts back to her mother tongue at 7 cm. *You see that a lot*, the midwife says, checking her screen.

The mother's body aches: pelvis, ankle, back, hip. The child does not care (sweet child, feral child), this child only wants to be carried – her little legs are tired, she is already bored on this so-very-expected planet.

The mother is heavy, each finger a two-litre carton of milk tied at the knuckle by a six-pack ring. She is nothing compared to the gravity of such a large planet. Her bones are pulped; she peeters out. Fuel – she's a fuel and it's burning. Strawberry sucked into a vacuum. Particles colliding near a greedy future. She remembers the slow calm of an empty afternoon. She does not read the news. None of it can (be allowed to) touch her.

The mother wants handles. Handles in cars, especially. She sits with her back firmly against the backrest. She wants handles on stairs, in chairs, mainly to get up out of them, and in fields, to help punctuate and withstand the distance. She wants to hold on, and to be held not held on to.

The mother swims underwater. She snatches at the toys young men in high chairs on the other side of the surface are dropping in to test her.

Her peripheral vision is shot. A mosaic of threat. Armada of rain or birds hitting glass. She has never seen a woodpecker (alive), phosphorescence, or the emerald calligraphy of a cold, thin night.

    The mother is waiting for the next needle to prick, the next bolt of static. She is the restless torpor of expecting to hear her own name. As she walks alone in some new city, she feels someone is going to catch her, know her, call her out.

        She needs hands all over this withdrawing body – endangered vultures to her ecosystem of meat.

            The mother is a bulb of tightness. She must close her eyes and let this succeed.

No, No, No

The flatness of rays, certain seeds, makes me want to
lie down. *I mowed this* – it's all we know. I creep under
doors. Flatpacked like housing, like furniture, like
drop a skinny burger between two lax lips.
We couldn't go to bed because we hadn't made it yet.
As people. My clothes are sobbing in the sink.
My intestines are soaking in the great sinkhole
of who I've tried to be. The tightness in my chest
feels like a newly imagined baby turning, knocking
down the atmosphere – it's not even any kind of fruit
yet and already I haven't enough in to breathe.

NERVES

Nerves: 2017

You snored, or coughed, I forget which, and in my half-sleep an angry dog jumped out of your mouth and into the middle of my face, where it stayed.

Nerves: 2021

I've started to flinch at amber lights. Unable to check my phone from the passenger side. Can't take my eyes off the road. Cars nosing into me, birds shrieking down, pedestrians lurching out. The drivers of these cars I'm in sigh-smile and *there-there* with the rules like I've been shying away my whole life.

I'm trying to explain the cars I've been in. The things I haven't noticed.

Eurghh, I croak several times per ride.

'Hard to imagine you as a driver.' 'I don't think you'd like driving.' 'You know, you'd make a terrible driver.' 'I reckon you'd storm the hazard awareness part of the theory test.' 'Ha, you can't go doing that if you want to drive.'

Nerves: Leeds

A crisp packet falls from its place in a cupboard. A low whirr along the canal. Movements in the flat downstairs climb into my arcades. Boys shout *knobhead* and wake up my baby // A man shouts *fuck off* to no one at 5 a.m., he's with no one, at the bus stop, beneath the open window of the room I am sleeping in. // I've had that in dreams before, my own voice berating me, but it's never been real. A suspicious silence follows.

Nerves: August

My man comes back. And instead of sleep I go out into the wild night. Instead of write I go out into the wild night. Instead of calm, I resist. It takes a while to set things right. My mother opens a packet of something and I jump to the side. Are you alright? I lie awake from 00:00 till 06:00, not able to sleep but at least nothing wants me. Alone with the traffic that drives through this glass, with the sporadic arm jumps of resting babies. The leg of the elder flips over and lands on the belly of the younger. I intermittently re-cover all those dreaming limbs. Though I don't know what they want, not really. I don't even know my own heart rate, how much REM I need, if this sweat is a chill, if this breeze is relief. The night passes like a comb and the day comes on like a revelation; it's a pleasure to have lived through it, and in such detail. My body fizzes.

Bypass

a stone in fruit / like so much bone / so much inflexible
protection / all I see are flexing biceps when I'm half asleep /
I've said to you / I shall still be many things / my hands
grasp like babies cling to worn cloth / dragging it off / and
the girl on the pier / held up the ex-crab / all limb to earth /
a shrug of shell / and the mother / hers / said show it to the
little girl / mine / and she did / and that was how we met /
we stare at skulls in the museum / there are still many
iterations of this self I have yet to assemble / never stop
dancing / on the dusk-shot rock / the breathy night / a
wave's fast camouflage / the flashing fins / a belly slap
disrupts your surface / a puff of smoke / one small party
popper forever floating on the ocean / we've had our fun /
somewhere in the middle of all this hardening / it's all I can
do / to repeat

MARCHING: A Diary (spring 2020)
or How hard it is to sustain a thing without belief

1/

I've been keeping a spreadsheet throughout these adjustments – acts of kindness, that sort of thing. It's hard to believe this is only day four. Hard to believe I wanted more time with my toddler and now that I've got it there's no one to share it with. Living in a country that is not mine I was always kind of hesitant in crowds, trying to second-guess which language I was about to be spoken to in. Now, there's hardly any social concern at all, no one's even looking each other in the eye. It's a communal spreadsheet, a shared document that I keep checking to see if anybody's playing with me. We went to the park. I know the quiet parts of the city. But when I tried to show my child the goats through the fencing she kept ramming her little bike against the gate, trying to get in. It's closed, I said. Daycare is closed. Your friends are at home too, I said, it's not just you. Come away from the gate.

2/

The centre of the city is hollowed out. An Easter egg cracked in two. I thought I'd be shocked but I've seen it all before, on the way to certain jobs, at the end of the forever-time of long nights out. Pigeons collect around the wheel of my bicycle, exponentially moving in. Iron filings with wings. I have nothing to give. Feelings of community dart from me like spider silk toward the other figures loitering, loose-limbed, at various points on the persistent cobbles. I want to drag them toward me and breathe in. I walk past my usual coffee place, now serving takeaway through a cat-flap, through the letterbox, through take-three- steps-back-and-we'll-open-and-retract, and I look inside. I wave at the owner and she waves back. Probably doesn't know who it is. A wave is a wave at the moment. She probably doesn't even care. The urge to throw myself on everyone. But this black hole around my legs and pulling me in. Prevalent thought: *We have no garden. They're going to lock us inside.* I'm at the office alone, pointlessly scanning. We are frozen in stone for a hundred years. Those that do move, like scavengers picking over the aftermath of a civilisation-long party. All of us evolving, becoming a turning point for whatever is after this. Sun through my window, taunting.

3/

It's the weekend. We cycle to some inconsequential ruins about an hour away and it feels like travel, until I realise it's that thinking-about-infinity trick that just loops back into more of the same. But it feels good to move my body, to fabricate such brief purpose. On the way back the wind is against us, I'm heading into dream clay. My pedals slow as the thickening days. From up on the dyke I see a horizon and push into that slowness. Seconds of distraction: a heron, a lake, a cloud, a burnt-out hotel, two crescent moons on an abandoned sign, sound of woodpecker, dash of rabbit, daffodil head in the hand of my child. A tired body is a peaceful body. Cheeks warm and red, lips cracked, pulsing. To return home again.

4/

Half-formed hours. A daily break from the living room means the afternoon isn't so long, the house isn't so small. Another cycle, long and guilty, but the child thinks everything is closed. She said to me this evening, *All the people have gone away.* I want to give her her friends again. This room isn't big enough to swing a mother in. Reassurance of neighbouring apartment lights lit late into the night. I want the sun, wind, plants unfurling over my passed-out body. Sweat and dew and mud and rain and all of it and everyone on top of me again. Silence on the bicycle lanes today, a lack of chatter, traffic. The week prepares to click over to Monday, like it matters. We need markers, laughter, we need to find the city's heart line. We need to find eye contact, new gestures. I want the distance to mean *I'm sorry* rather than *I am afraid*.

5/

The gulls are moving in. Dull crowds of pigeons circling as I courier past to deliver some books from work. Is this necessary? I need exercise, to be outside. Groups of people are either hanging around or they are not. Full sunlight, but under the underpass I'm feeling like I would feel at night. Still a man shouts at me for checking my phone while on the bike, to retain his sense of everything-I-know-is-right. Behave yourself, child. The lake is calm. So many woodpeckers. So glad we're all becoming the same. A slowness. Fear. Wonder. Where are our parents now? Distant, as always.

6/

How easy it is to slip into a thing, for the obscene to become routine. I stretch my back in the mornings, raise myself, raise my child. There are no morning alarms in this small world I am building; no straight path through a room, no right angles, no floor space, no surfaces that shine. Thick with contained life. Everything's coming in, the post, the food, all the emotions that should be released outside, toward other faces, but instead hit the computer screen and die. Every weekend we cycle to the factories, where smoke pumps the sky. It's reassuring to see momentum, industry, the ongoingness of things. We played on a scrap of grass, small canal overlooking a warehouse car park, oil trickling through reeds, drifting past the bluest of bottle tops. *I feel like all my life I've been building up to this*, she said into the screen. *And now it's here, I am at a complete loss*. The parks are full of people that appear to be making fun of me. I step outside, blink. I see queues at the supermarket, hear early-morning drunks shouting *rahh here I come* into all the nervous bodies waiting in a line. Trapped by habit, lack of planning. Nothing is certain but it is suspected that the root of the word *house*, of unknown origin, does indeed connect to the word *hide*.

7/

The slowness of confinement. The slowness of waking and within seconds being asked to play. My own moments becoming longer, asking for an elongate. Can I finish this drink? Can I finish this page? Can I stretch my back? Can I come round? Can I just lie here and wait? Then, at some point, the sun does shine brightly through the window and the day does say *come to me*, and my energy does reanimate. I can dress us, I say. This hunting of animals, any kind of movement an event on the bike lanes. But the highland cows were not there today. She was fishing in the river with a stick, pulling out bracken, blackened blades of grass and silt. I said be careful. It's what I always say. I did not want the mud on my face. I said be careful when she ran, but really it should have been my job to chase.

STUTTER

1.

I've brought my children to England for the summer. The older one and the newer one, both of whom were providing me with a different sort of agony from my position across the water. I say agony, but it's nothing much, an amount of loneliness, various kinds of suspected failure, theoretical and actual absences, time illuminated in the way only growing bodies can illuminate it, a rapid sprouting and leathering which shocks when binged on.

My bringing my children to England had, of course, nothing to do with my writing practice, though our being in England has every effect on how I practise my writing. I have relinquished half my parental support by leaving my partner on the other side of the water, waving us off as the clouds took my breath away. I wheeled the buggy and the mighty suitcase, my stretched arms tugging on handles, thinning like dough, ready to break, to be gathered up again and remade, displaying the creases and folds of my most recent fragmentation in their compacting.

I brought my children to England because there are more of them now, more than I ever could have imagined, and one was bulging out of me without a hook from the get-go. I have dreams of speed dating, so desperate am I for connection. In England, my children roll around in the soil, oiled in a language I have always known. Sweet children, lathered in thick chummy Lancashire vowels.

But I cannot write here. Every second is either too crucial or is not mine. Some of the seconds belong to my children, as a kind of investment, a longitudinal experiment that might if I'm lucky result in a friendship like no other I have ever known. I put in the work: work the land, feed the crop, till, tend, mow. I do not sing. Have never sang, not like a mother. If I sing, I sing like someone finally brave enough for karaoke; I sing like it's a warm evening and a warm crowd, using the fact my children are predisposed to like me as a way to unlock personal achievements. I do not sing for them, cannot hit those lull-me-to-sleep notes. Some of the seconds belong to my employer. These are the evenings (relax), the naps (sleep when your baby sleeps), the cartoons (educational tools), the bad parenting (lead by example), the foul moods (I am always in two rooms).

The boy interrupts me every thirty minutes this evening.

2.
I would love to remember the birth of my second child the way I remember the birth of my first; not that I've forgotten, but I haven't sat with it. Like a film watched half-heartedly and then forgotten (3 stars). I want to sit with the sensations and harbour new descriptions for them, synonyms of love, pain and endurance, instead of relying on the words spoken through the phone to whoever rang me at 3 a.m. that first morning. The nurse looking at me: this mother chatting away to a friend instead of coddling her newest newborn.

How little we know each other.

'We never get to speak,' I said to the nurse, unprompted. Three kids of her own. Almost impossible to catch her. Followed in my head by: *I don't live here I don't live here I want to go home.*

And so my baby waited – is waiting. Through the ins and outs of maternal strife, my easy exile, *trying not to lose oneself* in a world that assumes everything you have is what you always wanted because we don't tell one another otherwise. Snatch. Scavenge. Wring the neck of your own small life. Find what there is to find. Divide, divide.

3.

It was after having children that the desperation kicked in. Before that I was young, my path open to any kind of future. My way was messy, uncalibrated. Houses spilled people, jobs overlapped and underpaid. I was convinced that not becoming anything was a way of remaining possible – pregnant with opportunity.

I had my nose pierced at eleven, one tattoo when I was fifteen. Since then, nothing permanent. Dreams of squid and octopus constricting wrists, sperm whales scaling calves or forearms. First glimpsed, then doubted.

I was so much nothing that I flew in the slightest wind. I delighted in being told what to do with my time, in passively choosing which signage to claim. 'Ever heard of the Caucasus?' asked a period of my life I've later come to judge as circumspect, and I hadn't, so I hopped on the train. Missed the birth of a good friend's baby for that, the first of us to slip down the birth drain. Not through my own choice, you understand, but that of the strong male breeze into which I was caught.

And so it went for innumerable years. I waited to be whole. Being female, I waited for the wholeness to come to me, and when it did I followed. Definition seemed a threat. I had met

many men who didn't like tattoos (mine was small), or piercings (I wore a thin ring), or regional accents (I didn't speak), or certain styles of clothing (I can change). Imagine if that was your true love, just there, but you'd foolishly cut in a fringe. Better to be a blank but interesting slate.
Entrepreneurial in my enthusiasms with a history both virgin and verdant. Enough life experience to hold my own, but when it came to having held the private land of others it was best to have left no trace.

I was going to be a writer. If you'd asked me then, I would have said there was time enough further down the line. That first I'll live. In truth, what I didn't want was to be laughed at. Old men laughing. Old females sitting next to old males laughing. Young men scoffing and realising their mistake. Young females saying, 'Oh, is that about your earache?'

Like with language, when a child learns, we encourage, when a child errs, we show a better way. Up until a certain point we delight in being masters; the children are cute, the baby plants with their tiny leaves paired like open hands. But after a while, we've said it already, moved on. Some other sparkling bone has our attention now, the way it eddies in the water. The children are missing teeth, they stink; what we took as their beauty is asymmetrical now, has spread into difficult nuance. The plants are blocking the sunlight, riddled with aphids. We can't leave the windows open because the unkempt ends of vines are sprawling in. After a certain age, what you haven't learned will not be freely given. You will have to wade.

There are supermarket trolleys in the water, bikes all ribboned up to the gears with river weeds. I muddy myself in the many channels. Learn the green and grey of brick, the tide, the water level. I come to know what to expect, the sounds that signal a boat about to pass overhead, the lifting of a bridge and the queues that form during its upending.

If you'd asked me then, I would have said I was free. Yet my clothes were damp and smelled of sulphur. Many places I would never have attempted to enter would, if I had, quite promptly turned me away. But I was free to touch brick, I was free to exit and enter the water, or pitch a tent beneath the nearest tree. I was free to either go or not go to work, and free enough to turn up, if I did, in whatever state I so wished. I had whims, feet, and this supposed potential I carried around like a flame in wind.

Whenever a bold man, liking the look of me, said 'come here', I more or less did.

And often, in my unwholeness, the meteor hit.

Lost in perpetual self-blitz, I want to be nothing, beautiful silence, unforded fjord, eternal prospect, shimmering like an ore in carbon. Shuffling about in my under-the-earth seat. Hand in the air like an eager schoolchild, but not, because I never did, instead sitting on my fingers, begging them to hold it in until later, much later, screaming 'pick me, pick me!'

Since having children, I write when I can. Gone are the days I thought a voice had to be mature in order to speak.

Since having children I write when I can, like now when my mother and my baby could shriek through the door (I've locked it) at any moment.

'A few hours', she said. What has it been?

There is no time for doubt. Babies pull my legs below the surface. There is no time for any of the things I might yet or never will be. I grab an anchor, any anchor, a kite tail, the final carriage of a moving vehicle. I hope my knuckles are up to it, my calluses. I hold on to the zipline.

I go down the slide, massive and joyful. 'My children!' I scream. 'Carry me!'

4.
Recurring dream of being asked to speak. Being called out from the cornfield. I didn't mean to enter the race, but you itch. The itch runs down your arms, your torso, you can't exist without your body refracting light, however dim. And the proof is there, in the pedestrians stepping aside, in the doorway that closes on your lazy fingers holding the hinge, in the rain that hits and slips along your head and thorax and abdomen. Your lumpy presence unfolds, shakes out vestiges of wings. Vacuum pack unsealed. Cheap tent dismantled. You'll never get the thing back in.

The silence of my external surface. A semi-private channel, free as one's thoughts, is threading through me and my hands allow the drip to settle on the phone screen.

5.
Motherhood is fragmentation. I'll give nothing up. Take this prose poem and this and this. Wring it. Fold and stretch and stitch. There are caverns of salt, stalactites to swing from. The drip-drip of nipping earth teeth. Take a spoonful of night-middle and squeeze. All the little dogs are sleeping, one cough and they'll start pulling on the reins.

Motherhood is ekphrasis. I'm responding to unprocessed images, sometimes from months ago. Fill myself up, fly through the days, sleep, and repeat. Later, in the shreds of solitude, my literary Cheestrings, I'll try to remember. I fluff up the couscous, plump the pillow, dig deep into the polystyrene snow to find the abandoned paperweight. Dandelion clock blown into fossil. The soft made hard. Still. Still easy to see. Rotated time, examined. The opposite of a blink.

Motherhood is constraint. Teeth marks line the tongue, an uneven ridge. The heart stops to listen. A summons? A body that doesn't understand height and doesn't know where it sleeps. The seeking of a mouth, a barnacle chiselled off and flung seeks to reconnect, GSOH. I push my hands to the seabed as a freak wave takes off my head.

Motherhood is a language. Whatever she said first is how I also say it. She leads me to the middle sense. Not wanting to correct. The poetry of a life spent in prenatal waters. Open the flap and spot five differences: one is you and one is me.

Motherhood is collage, found art at the flea market. A photo book that says *Married for 50 Years* is seen under the bridge in the park; is too big to carry, is taken by another, worked with. I cut out the animals, try to show her how we all connect, make every doodle a feminist text. I tell her what *mistaken* means but she says she doesn't like the sound. The *m* and the *k*, she says, not together, no. She doesn't like it. I ask her if she likes *milk*, or *makkelijk*, the Dutch word for *easy*. She does, yes, and now doesn't know what her stance is. I send her on paths, she sends me on paths, taking our lives out to play.

Motherhood is juxtaposition, a tectonic jolt. Territories that don't add up either side of the water. A spinal stretch toward the light, each planet a cupboard one cupboard too high. Better the cloud, the lazy forms, the slap-slap-slap of a dull coast.

Motherhood is a manifesto I have yet to write.

6.
This truck of noise is continuously placing me on and ramming me off the road. My babies are sliding down the cliff and my only job is to reach out and hoist them.

Two sirens are going off at the same time like broken toys, failing batteries lurch-sounding through the night. Smoke alarms remind us to change them, change them, change them or quietly die.

What do you do to unwind? I lie on the floor when I find some, when I find the time, and try to be long like before. Press my back and neck to the carpet. I stare at the calmness of ceiling lights. Such precise starlight. Smoothest plaster.

I stand with my feet in the hot water and cry at the silhouetted mountain so purely black against the shifty twilight, imagine a human shape walking along the fragment of button moon circumference, the peppa pig hill ridge. My body is a tiny starfish in the darkness, a deep-time octopus leg, each bone dancing on the twig of the previous, bonelet on bonestem. My navel hoovers up all of the moon and the stars and the never-ending space dust.

7.

I spend another sleepless night, turning left, turning right. The gentle body, the cool romperless midriff. The skin trusts like charcoal does on paper, the smooth bold change from a previous state. This baby is a smudge, an oval, its head a priceless pebble, a Baoding ball protecting the almighty capital.

I turn away, babies all along my back and then some. A tide of babies. My bumpy horizon. Thoughts loop around in a sea of swirling plastic. The good conscious, the bad conscious, faces coming to fruition and receding behind a cloud of pollution. Brain fog, they call it. Post-something. Meta-motherhood. Remember thoughts, assigning nouns. I called my child 'Toilet' earlier. Shouted it across the cafe clear as day. She knew where we were going, what I was after. The truth was in the voice. Sentences are as malleable as sentences. My knees break. Sense is in the time of the beholder. I curl up on the swing bed and persuade the world to rotate.

GRAVEYARD SHIFT
(please remember me)

1.
Pillows part, my body
slips into the gap. Pieces of
fabric, flaps of skin, small nails
clutching. We stretch
and fold like dough turning over,
our borders shift, cloud
formations between blinks.
Uncertain feathers line my lips,
my eyelids the static of rubbed balloons
– a no man's strip
between me and this new moon.
Sweat sticks.
This cat-purr baby is not
yet the future. There is still time
for all of this.

2.
Let me rest, but please
breathe. Don't ever stop,
we won't ever stop.
You're a small cushion
on the pile, alive
in the middle
of so much
upholstery. Hold me
up, help me
face life.

3.
Evening light, small
neon flecks at the filling station
sway from side to side
in the loaded silence that is
this and every night.
Hydraulic release of
your breath, the let-down
of our two vehicles: my attention
turns to your relaxed
suspension, your pearl of head. Your
binary mouth. My implosion
of worth now crushed
to some essential diamond.
This orbital putting on and taking off,
this key in the ignition that fits
but just won't turn. We scramble
through unfurling sheets
in never-ending instruction. Lead
to this assembly of bed.

4.
A scream itches round from beyond the door,
uncoupled from this small throat
I am inhaling. I don't know
which of my babies is in my arms.
What new mass is this? What body
am I to love? What night? Waves lash
against the rock. How exquisite it is
to shore. We detail the photographs
we have lost, the light. This new ritual
involves so much parting, so much flair.

5.
Small barnacle mouths
scour the surface of my rocks
for food. A symbiotic washing
of skins. A return flight
as what passes from me
passes also from him.
The plane doesn't land,
only circles in the polar night.
I have never been searched like this.

6.
Electricity pylons unfold,
accordions across untamed land.
Buzzing paper dolls, beacons
of life. Echoes of you
that were,
that were,
that were. Your features in flux
with every blink, every trick
of the light. And my eyes poor witnesses
to the rotations of the night
where for small moments we align
as we lie side by side
in mutual fright.

7.
Roots like this clump of hair you climb
knot between your fingers and pull me
down to eyelashes long as spider limbs
or crane flies darting to and from the twigs
of shaven trees that scratch against our daybreak
harbour and all the little fur upon your shoulders
and this feed and all your backwash and your hair
falling out and my hair falling out and this dummy
covered in moult from fabric and this one long hair
of mine caught in that mouth that is always open
and always gathering dust from me.

    Our bamboo bodies are talking. Coiled
messages shoot through the void. Soil comes
loose around tender tendrils that are rooting
for you. For me.

8.
Etc. and our rounds of careful torchlight.
Sharp beams of the day's shrapnel
stream in across the shallows
of our ceiling street lights. Where motorbikes,
where rogue elements breaking curfew
are newly appointed lighting technicians
for our determined
whirlwind. We breach, flip, and,
blowholes panting, plunge home
through the shatterglass
surface. We are not broken,
only cubed. Dispersed
throughout the crowd,
that is, the barren ocean.

9.
Mammal-happy in the unsleep,
we lunge toward the other,
one stooped, one stretched.
Our bodies bear witness
to the eradication of the distance
between us. Like the marks left
on skin when clothing is removed.

10.
Excavated, what sweet treasure
was removed. How it illuminates
the skittish fragments
of my former dips and dives
around the human centres. How it roots
through mud and rock and earth
to cast me in such pale opal.

11.
Mothers drop from the walls like milk
from teats; first one small fish, then two, three,
then larger fish, crustaceans, pinnipeds,
thickets of trembling kelp. The flood.
Our heads up at the ceiling, grazing –
mouths of tiny birds. I want to be fed.
Want nest. To sink into loose hay,
drift into fodder. So convenient, this softness,
no need to chew. Your piranha mouth snaps
me back into the room.

12.
Babystar orbits this old giant
in turn orbiting its own bright spot
of celestial quiver. Babycentre lives
in the mass of the mother, both are
pulled toward the limits of her surface.
One body crawls around the other,
claws at her dust. Bats at her passing
asteroid futures. *Oumuamua*, it cries. Yes?
You're sailing away at the speed of light.

13.
End of the night shift and the sky
is pink, your cheeks. Faint blush of planet
from behind a whorl of streets. We were,
you will be. The observable universe
contracts to the peak of these fresh sheets,
lies flush over my raised right knee.
And I've forgotten to blink, my eyes red
as your tender skin, my tear ducts
working to blur this precious moment
as I apply the automatic cream.

14.
Remember me in the dream spill,
loose as I became as I shared out my body.
As I became the plughole, the plug,
and also the drain. This sewer is the stream
of our weeks and we flow along
with all the leftover waste of the past
stomping around above this site
of our hurried labour. We climb,
poke our heads out these small hills
we've made. The street is on fire,
seismic cracks stripe my belly
and with every step we are sent
back down into the tunnels.
Our narrow and parallel dormitories.
From the smallness of our night
tables we exchange notes.

15.
My son is unfolding,
anonymous. There are wires,
vines, tangled threads that hook
him up to the wider world.
He's flailing in the dark, limbs
like experimental plants in cupboards,
limbs like exemplary plants in cupboards
attesting to the presence
of unproven gods. And our own minds
still too fresh to comprehend it. Upside-down
beetles, tortoise shells, tipped cows. We tumble
together through this necessary interruption.

16.
Endless gravity, tiny ropes
and their million-point tugging
like pinpoint pricks of Lilliput night.
My spread-eagled body and a world
of veins from me to the million stars.
Grass is growing over me: I am
lagoon, oasis. Animals crawl up
and over my this-and-that dunes.
I have been here forever, waiting.

Acknowledgments

The prologue is adapted from an editorial written for Versal's live bi-monthly poetry evenings in Amsterdam.

Thanks to Ian Seed for publishing Specific Ways I Will Apologise to My Children on The Fortnightly Review, to Gregory and Susanna of Abridged, where Shut Up and Drive was first published, and to Melissa Severin for her ruthless editing. In the Cornfield was originally published by J A Tyler on the now-defunct Mud Luscious Press website, and was one of the first pieces I ever had published.

Large portions of this book were written in my mother's flat as she watched Emmerdale.

Graveyard Shift was written in January/February 2021, while breastfeeding, between 1 and 4 a.m.

LYDIA UNSWORTH's latest collection is *Mortar* (Osmosis Press). Pamphlets include *These Steady Bulbs* and *Residue* (above/ground), *cement, terraces* (Red Ceilings), and *YIELD* (KFS). Work can be found in places like Ambit, Banshee, Bath Magg, Blackbox Manifold, The Interpreter's House, Oxford Poetry, Shearsman, SPAM, and Tentacular. Her forthcoming collection, Arthropod, will be published by Death of Workers Whilst Building Skyscrapers in 2024.

www.ingramcontent.com/pod-product-compliance
Lightning Source LLC
Chambersburg PA
CBHW030228100526
44585CB00012BA/432